THE OFFICIAL

POKÉMON

Handbook #3

Scholastic Inc.

New York   Toronto   London   Auckland   Sydney
Mexico City   New Delhi   Hong Kong   Buenos Aires

To Julie, Barry Jr., and Tiffany, thank you
for introducing me to the World of Pokémon.

Joshua would like to thank his parents, for
encouraging his creative imagination, and secondly
his fiancée, Bridget, for continuing where his parents
left off, and loving him for the really big kid that he is.

Acknowledgments
Thank you for your help:
Susan Simpson, Maria Barbo,
Wally Cabrera, Randi Reisfeld,
Ellie Berger, and Susan Eisner.

Edited by: Stephanie Howze, Joshua Izzo and Tina Painton
Designed by: Sabrina Sevilla

ISBN 0-439-31747-9

12 11 10 9 8 7 6 5 4 3 2 1   1 2 3 4 5 6

Printed in the U.S.A.

First Scholastic printing, September 2001

A WORD FROM PROFESSOR OAK

Greetings, Pokémon trainers! I am Professor Oak, a Pokémon scientist. I spend my time studying and learning about Pokémon and how they behave.

I have even more exciting news to share with you. Remember in *Handbook #2* when I gave aspiring Pokémon trainers a sneak peek from my secret files about what you can expect from the rest of the new Pokémon? Well, the wait is over! That's right! The next level of Pokémon is here and it is definitely all that!

Pokémon experts like myself need your help to learn everything we can about these new and unusual Pokémon. We have already gathered much useful information about the new starter Pokémon like Totodile, Chikorita, and Cyndaquil, but there is still a lot to be discovered about the Electric Pichu brothers, the amazing abilities of Ursaring, and why Tyranitar is called the armor Pokémon. That's why it is so important for you to keep updating your Pokédex.

Your Official Pokémon Handbook #3: Gold and Silver Edition promises to give you the scoop, the whole scoop and nothing but the scoop on all new Pokémon. It's everything you'll need to know to spot, catch, and train these unique new Pokémon.

Your mission: Continue to work hard at becoming the best Pokémon trainer you can be. If you haven't already, you may even find some never—before—seen Pokémon of your own.

Read up. Stock up on Poké Balls. And catch 'em all!

—Professor Oak

Who's That Pokémon?

Get ready for evolution next — some of the brand-new Pokémon are evolutions of some of the original 150 Pokémon.

Thought Chansey and Scyther never changed? Guess again. They evolve into Blissey and Scizor. Thought Slowpoke could only evolve into Slowbro? Now we know that if Shellder clamps onto Slowpoke's head instead of its tail, Slowpoke will evolve into the brand-new, super-smart Pokémon, Slowking.

Ready for another surprise? Some of the new Pokémon are pre-evolutions of original Pokémon. That means the new Pokémon came first. New Pokémon Elekid actually evolves into Electabuzz. Recently discovered Cleffa evolves into Clefairy. The just found Igglybuff evolves into favorite Pokémon songster, Jigglypuff! And the egg-shell Pokémon Togepi evolves into Togetic!

EVOLUTION

Just like people, Pokémon don't stay the same forever. As they learn and grow, most Pokémon change form. They evolve! Most Pokémon go through one or two evolutions. After a while, Pokémon stop evolving — but they never stop learning and getting stronger.

There are two basic ways a Pokémon can evolve or change form:

1) **With experience.** With good training, Pokémon can learn new attacks and defense moves to get stronger and smarter. The more a Pokémon competes, the more it will learn and the quicker it will evolve.

2) **With special stones.** Some Pokémon cannot evolve without special stones like the Moon Stone or Thunder Stone. Once you have the stone, you can use it to evolve your Pokémon whenever you want.

New Poké Balls!
Get in Gear!

Don't forget to stock up on Poké Balls before heading out on your training journey. You'll need them to catch new Pokémon.

There are lots of cool new Poké Balls out there, but the most mysterious is the GS Ball. Unlike regular Poké Balls, which are red and white, this ball is gold on top and silver on bottom. Professor Oak received the ball from his friend Professor Ivy, who lives in the Orange Islands. Professor Oak sent young Pokémon trainer Ash Ketchum to Professor Ivy's lab on Valencia Island to pick it up.

Why didn't Professor Ivy just transport the ball to Professor Oak's lab like a regular Poké Ball? Can't be done. And what's even stranger? No one can figure out how to open the GS Ball! Professor Ivy and her assistants tried using buzz saws, hammers, crowbars, hacksaws, power drills, and lasers. Nothing worked. So no one knows what is inside.

No one even knows who made it or why. So, Ash is on a new mission to take the ball to a famous Poké Ball designer named Kurt. He's from Azalea Town in the western territories.

What mysteries does the GS Ball hold? Could a never-before-seen Pokémon be inside? Will you be the Pokémon trainer who reveals the mystery of the GS Ball?

Poké Ball Power

Poké Balls are what you carry your Pokémon around in while you are training them. Only one Pokémon fits in each ball. You can also use Poké Balls to catch wild Pokémon. Different Poké Balls work best to catch different Pokémon. Choose which Poké Ball you will use depending on the situation you face.

Some Pokémon are common. There are tons of Mareep. But other Pokémon, like Ho-oh and Lugia, are so rare, there is only one of each.

New Pokémon Eggs

Did you know that Togepi is not the only Pokémon that hatched from an egg? Now, there are more! Here's what you need to know about them.

How do you get a new, young Pokémon? Just leave a boy and girl of the same Pokémon at the nearest Pokémon Breeding Center for a while. (Yes — Pokémon can be male or female.) When you return you'll have a brand-new Pokémon. For example, bring in two Jigglypuff, two Electabuzz, or two Clefairy, and head home with a new Igglybuff, Elekid, or Cleffa.

Take note: This might not work with all Pokémon, so get the details before you leave your Pokémon at any breeding center.

No breeding center nearby? Maybe you'll be lucky enough to find a Pokémon egg. Then you can hatch it yourself — just like Ash Ketchum and his friends did with the Togepi egg they found in Grandfather Canyon.

New Type: Dark

Up until now there have been fifteen different types of Pokémon — Bug, Dragon, Electric, Fighting, Fire, Flying, Ghost, Grass, Ground, Ice, Normal, Poison, Psychic, Rock, and Water.
Get ready for this — there are two brand-new types of Pokémon, Steel and Dark. When Eevee evolves at night, the result is Umbreon, a Dark type Pokémon. Umbreon is a very useful Pokémon with great defense skills. It would make a great addition to any Pokémon team.

HEADS UP: Team Rocket has been known to scam Pokémon trainers by pretending to run phony breeding centers. Trainers drop off their Pokémon, and when they come back to pick them up — the entire center is gone and their beloved Pokémon are being shipped off to Giovanni, head of the evil Team Rocket enterprise.

The Johto Journeys

As you've seen, the world of Pokémon just got bigger. There are new lands to explore, new adventures to be had, and new badges to win. Many of the new Pokémon have been spotted in the western territories, just west of Pallet Town. If you want to check out the latest and greatest in the world of Pokémon, head west young Pokémon trainer and take a Johto journey.

The Western Territories Have a League of Their Own: The Johto League

If you want to be a licensed Pokémon trainer, you have to compete in a Pokémon League. The league sets the rules of battle, and gives each trainer his/her first Pokémon and a Pokédex. Each league has its own set of rules, different lands to explore, and different badges to earn. Trainers earn badges by competing in Pokémon battles in gyms all over the world.

There are two main leagues — the Indigo League and the Johto League. The Indigo League is the most well-known of all Pokémon Leagues. Many trainers start out in this league. These trainers compete in gyms in towns and cities like Cerulean City and Cinnabar Island in the lands east of the Indigo Plateau.

The second league is the Johto League. New trainers starting their Pokémon journeys in the western territories can sign up to compete in this league. All they have to do is register at the Pokémon Center in New Bark Town. Then they can pick up their very first Pokémon at the lab of Professor Elm. The Johto League territory begins where the Indigo League territory ends — just west of the Indigo Plateau. Can't decide which league is right for you? You can compete in both. Once you have earned badges in one league, you can travel to the other one and compete for new badges in new lands.

Badge Blowout

No matter what Pokémon League you join, you will earn a badge each time you defeat a Gym Leader in competition. The rules for earning badges vary from league to league and sometimes from gym to gym. But one thing remains the same: A badge is an important sign of your skill as a Pokémon trainer. It shows that you know enough about Pokémon to defeat a skilled trainer in a one-on-one competition. It also shows that your Pokémon are willing to step up to the plate for you. It's a sign that you've earned their respect and friendship.

The Winner's Cup

The Indigo and Johto Leagues aren't the only Pokémon Leagues around. The Orange Islands have a Pokémon League as well. If a trainer earns four badges in the Orange League and goes on to win the championship tournament, that trainer takes home the Orange League Winner's Cup.

How does the Johto League match up to the Indigo League?

Many trainers starting out in the **INDIGO LEAGUE** begin their journeys at Professor Oak's lab in Pallet Town. There, they can choose their first Pokémon from:

Bulbasaur
#01
Grass and Poison Type

Charmander
#04
Fire Type

Squirtle
#07
Water Type

Many trainers in the **JOHTO LEAGUE** begin their journeys at Professor Elm's lab in New Bark Town. They can choose to start out with:

Chikorita
#152
Grass Type

Cyndaquil
#155
Fire Type

Totodile
#158
Water Type

BADGE	JOHTO LEAGUE	INDIGO LEAGUE
Number of badges to earn	At least 8	At least 8
Eight badges qualifies trainers to battle in:	The Johto League Championship	The Pokémon League Tournament
Pokémon gyms:	Trainers battle for badges like the ZephyrBadge and the Hive Badge in places like Violet City Gym and Azalea Town Gym.	Trainers battle for badges like the Cascade Badge and Earth Badge in places like the Cerulean City Gym or the Viridian City Gym.

With all the experience you gain competing in either the Johto League or the Indigo League, you're sure to become a Pokémon Master in no time!

INDIGO BADGES

Cascade Boulder Soul Rainbow Earth Marsh Thunder Volcano

JOHTO BADGES

Fog Glacier Mineral Zephyr Storm Rising Hive Plain

TYPE CASTING

Every Pokémon has a type — like Grass, Water, and Fire. Type tells you a lot about a Pokémon, including what moves it will use in battle, and where it likes to live. For example, Fire Pokémon usually enjoy hot, dry places like volcanoes. They may use attacks such as Flame-thrower or Fire Spin. Grass Pokémon prefer to get tons of sunlight. Grass Types use attacks like Vine Whip and Razor Leaf.

Type also helps you figure out which kind of Pokémon will do well in a battle against another type. Water dampens Fire, and Fire scorches Grass. Flying Types have an advantage over Ground Types. But Ground Types take the charge out of Electric Types.

There are now seventeen different types.

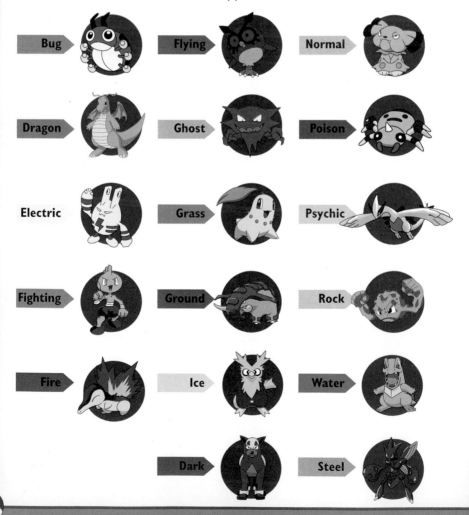

WHAT'S YOUR TYPE?

When Pokémon trainers like Ash Ketchum are going for a badge or facing off against another trainer, they think about which type of Pokémon might do well against their opponent's Pokémon. Use this chart as a quick guide to Pokémon type.

FIRE

#04 CHARMANDER™ #58 GROWLITHE™ #126 MAGMAR™ #157 TYPHLOSION™

#05 CHARMELEON™ #59 ARCANINE™ #136 FLAREON™ #218 SLUGMA™

#37 VULPIX™ #77 PONYTA™ #155 CYNDAQUIL™ #240 MAGBY™

#38 NINETALES™ #78 RAPIDASH™ #156 QUILAVA™ #244 ENTEI™

TYPES

ELECTRIC

 #25 PIKACHU™

 #172 PICHU™

#26 RAICHU™

#179 MAREEP™

 #100 VOLTORB™

#180 FLAAFFY™

 #101 ELECTRODE™

#181 AMPHAROS™

#125 ELECTABUZZ™

#239 ELEKID™

#135 JOLTEON™

#243 RAIKOU™

POISON

 #23 EKANS™

 #33 NIDORINO™

#24 ARBOK™

#88 GRIMER™

 #29 NIDORAN™ ♀

 #89 MUK™

 #30 NIDORINA™

 #109 KOFFING™

 #32 NIDORAN™ ♂

 #110 WEEZING™

BUG

 #10 CATERPIE™

#127 PINSIR™

#11 METAPOD™

 #204 PINECO™

 12

TYPES

PSYCHIC

#63 ABRA™

#150 MEWTWO™

#64 KADABRA™

#151 MEW™

#65 ALAKAZAM™

#196 ESPEON™

#96 DROWZEE™

#201 UNOWN™

#97 HYPNO™

#202 WOBBUFFET™

#122 MR. MIME™

GROUND

#27 SANDSHREW™

#104 CUBONE™

#28 SANDSLASH™

#105 MAROWAK™

#50 DIGLETT™

#231 PHANPY™

#51 DUGTRIO™

#232 DONPHAN™

GRASS

#152 CHIKORITA™

#182 BELLOSSOM™

#153 BAYLEEF™

#191 SUNKERN™

#114 TANGELA™

#154 MEGANIUM™

#192 SUNFLORA™

TYPES

NORMAL

 #19 RATTATA™

 #108 LICKITUNG™

 #161 SENTRET™

 #216 TEDDIURSA™

 #20 RATICATE™

 #113 CHANSEY™

 #162 FURRET™

 #217 URSARING™

 #35 CLEFAIRY™

 #115 KANGASKHAN™

 #174 IGGLYBUFF™

 #233 PORYGON2™

 #36 CLEFABLE™

 #128 TAUROS™

#175 TOGEPI™

#234 STANTLER™

 #39 JIGGLYPUFF™

#132 DITTO™

 #190 AIPOM™

 #235 SMEARGLE™

 #40 WIGGLYTUFF™

#133 EEVEE™

 #206 DUNSPARCE™

 #241 MILTANK™

 #52 MEOWTH™

#137 PORYGON™

 #209 SNUBBULL™

 #242 BLISSEY™

 #53 PERSIAN™

 #143 SNORLAX™

 #210 GRANBULL™

TYPES

WATER

#07 SQUIRTLE™

#90 SHELLDER™

#129 MAGIKARP™

#184 AZUMARILL™

#08 WARTORTLE™

#98 KRABBY™

#134 VAPOREON™

#186 POLITOED™

#09 BLASTOISE™

#99 KINGLER™

#158 TOTODILE™

#223 REMORAID™

#54 PSYDUCK™

#116 HORSEA™

#159 CROCONAW™

#224 OCTILLERY™

#55 GOLDUCK™

#117 SEADRA™

#160 FERALIGATR™

#245 SUICUNE™

#60 POLIWAG™

#118 GOLDEEN™

#183 MARILL™

#61 POLIWHIRL™

#119 SEAKING™

GHOST

#86 SEEL™

#120 STARYU™

#200 MISDREAVUS™

TYPES

FIGHTING

 #56 MANKEY™

#67 MACHOKE™

#107 HITMONCHAN™

#57 PRIMEAPE™

#68 MACHAMP™

#236 TYROGUE™

 #66 MACHOP™

#106 HITMONLEE™

#237 HITMONTOP™

DRAGON

 #147 DRATINI™

#148 DRAGONAIR™

BUG/ ROCK

 #213 SHUCKLE™

ROCK

 #185 SUDOWOODO™

DARK

#197 UMBREON™

BUG/ POISON

 #13 WEEDLE™

 #14 KAKUNA™

 #15 BEEDRILL™

#48 VENONAT™

 #49 VENOMOTH™

#167 SPINARAK™

#168 ARIADOS™

TYPES

GRASS/ FLYING

#187 HOPPIP™

#188 SKIPLOOM™

#189 JUMPLUFF™

BUG/ FLYING

#12 BUTTERFREE™

#123 SCYTHER™

#163 LEDYBA™

#166 LEDIAN™

#193 YANMA™

GRASS/ POISON

#01 BULBASAUR™

#43 ODDISH™

#69 BELLSPROUT™

#02 IVYSAUR™

#44 GLOOM™

#70 WEEPINBELL™

#03 VENUSAUR™

#45 VILEPLUME™

#71 VICTREEBEL™

DRAGON/ FLYING

#149 DRAGONITE™

ELECTRIC/ FLYING

#145 ZAPDOS™

BUG/ STEEL

#212 SCIZOR™

#205 FORRETRESS™

TYPES

NORMAL/ FLYING

#16 PIDGEY™

#21 SPEAROW™

#84 DODUO™

#164 NOCTOWL™

#17 PIDGEOTTO™

#22 FEAROW™

#85 DODRIO™

#176 TOGETIC™

#18 PIDGEOT™

#83 FARFETCH'D™

#163 HOOTHOOT™

FIRE/ FLYING

#06 CHARIZARD™

#146 MOLTRES™

#250 HO-OH™

ICE/ FLYING

#144 ARTICUNO™

GHOST/ POISON

#92 GASTLY™

#93 HAUNTER™

#94 GENGAR™

#225 DELIBIRD™

TYPES

GROUND/ FLYING

#207 GLIGAR™

ROCK/ WATER

#138 OMANYTE™

#141 KABUTOPS™

#139 OMASTAR™

#222 CORSOLA™

#140 KABUTO™

ROCK/ FLYING

#142 AERODACTYL™

ORASS/ PSYCHIC

#102 EXEGGCUTE™   #103 EXEGGUTOR™

ICE/ PSYCHIC

#124 JYNX™   #238 SMOOCHUM™

PSYCHIC/ FLYING

#177 NATU™   #178 XATU™   #249 LUGIA™

NORMAL/ PSYCHIC

#203 GIRAFARIG™

TYPES

DARK/ ICE
#215 SNEASEL™

FIRE/ ROCK
#219 MAGCARGO™

DARK/ FLYING
#198 MURKROW™

DARK/ FIRE
#228 HOUNDOUR™

#229 HOUNDOOM™

BUG/ GRASS
#46 PARAS™

#47 PARASECT™

ELECTRIC/ STEEL
#81 MAGNEMITE™

#82 MAGNETON™

POISON/ FLYING
#41 ZUBAT™

#42 GOLBAT™

#169 CROBAT™

DARK/ ROCK
#248 TYRANITAR™

TYPES

ROCK/ GROUND

#74 GEODUDE™ #111 RHYHORN™

#75 GRAVELER™ #112 RHYDON™

#76 GOLEM™ #246 LARVITAR™

#95 ONIX™ #247 PUPITAR™

STEEL/ FLYING

#227 SKARMORY™

STEEL/ GROUND

#208 STEELIX™

WATER/ GROUND

#195 QUAGSIRE™

#194 WOOPER™

POISON/ GROUND

#31 NIDOQUEEN™

#34 NIDOKING™

ICE/ GROUND

#220 SWINUB™

#221 PILOSWINE™

TYPES

WATER/ POISON

#72 TENTACOOL™ #73 TENTACRUEL™ #211 QWILLFISH™

WATER/ FIGHTING

#62 POLIWRATH™

WATER/ DRAGON

#230 KINGDRA™

WATER/ ICE

#87 DEWGONG™ #91 CLOYSTER™ #131 LAPRAS™

WATER/ FLYING

#130 GYARADOS™ #226 MANTINE™

WATER/ ELECTRIC

#170 CHINCHOU™ #171 LANTURN™

WATER/ PSYCHIC

#79 SLOWPOKE™ #80 SLOWBRO™ #121 STARMIE™ #199 SLOWKING™

It's time for a Pokédex Upgrade

NEW

Pokémon experts like Professor Oak have updated your Pokédex. It's got new information and a brand-new look. Use it as a quick guide to help you train your Pokémon.

A Pokédex is a handheld computer that contains everything you need to know about Pokémon. Every time you spot a new Pokémon, your Pokédex will have the INFO to describe the Pokémon's character, abilities, and where the Pokémon likes to live.

#152 CHIKORITA™
LEAF Pokémon

How to say it:
Chick-ore-EEE-tah

Type:
Grass

Height:
2' 11"

Weight:
14 lbs.

Attacks:
**TACKLE, GROWL,
RAZOR LEAF, REFLECT,
POISON POWDER**

Evolution:
**Chikorita evolves
into Bayleef.**

Chikorita is one of the three starter Pokémon of the Johto League. The sweet-smelling leaves that grow from its body can be used for a devastating Razor Leaf Attack. Chikorita are known for being very docile and they just love to go out into the sun and soak up some rays!

Pokédex Pick:

In the Kanto League, new trainers can pick three starter Pokémon — Chamander, a Fire Pokémon; Bulbasaur, a Grass Pokémon; and Squirtle, a Water Pokémon. In the Johto League new trainers get to choose from Chikorita, a Grass Pokémon; Cyndaquil, a Fire Pokémon or Totodile, a Water Pokémon.

#153 BAYLEEF™
LEAF Pokémon

How to say it:
BAY-leef

Type: Grass

Height: 3' 11"

Weight: 35 lbs.

Attacks:
RAZOR LEAF, REFLECT, POISON POWDER, SYNTHESIS, BODY SLAM

Evolution:
Bayleef evolves into Meganium.

Bayleef is the second stage of evolution for Chikorita. When you're around a Bayleef you'll probably notice a sweet, spicy scent wafting in the air. The newly evolved Bayleef emanates the aroma from the leaves around its neck. The aroma acts as a stimulant to restore health. Somehow, sniffing it also makes Pokémon want to fight.

#154 MEGANIUM™
HERB Pokémon

Meganium is the third and final evolutionary form of Chikorita and Bayleef. Unlike its younger, pre-evolved form of Bayleef, the aroma that wafts from Meganium petals has the ability to calm and soothe angry feelings. This gentle Pokémon not only has the power to calm down aggression, but its breath has the power to bring dead flowers and grass back to life!

How to say it:
Muh-gay-knee-um

Type: Grass

Height: 5' 11"

Weight: 222 lbs.

Attacks:
TACKLE, GROWL, RAZOR LEAF, SYNTHESIS, BODY SLAM, LIGHT SCREEN, SAFEGUARD, SOLARBEAM

Evolution:
Meganium is the evolved form of Chikorita and Bayleef.

#155 CYNDAQUIL™
FIRE MOUSE Pokémon

How to say it:
SIN-da-qwil

Type: Fire

Height: 1' 08"

Weight: 17 lbs.

Attacks:
TACKLE, LEER,
SMOKESCREEN,
EMBER

Evolution:
Cyndaquil evolves
into Quilava.

This fiery little Pokémon is one of the new three starter Pokémon that new trainers can get at the beginning of the Johto Journey. If you have Cyndaquil, don't be surprised if it remains in a hunched over position or curls-up into a little ball. Also take care not to scare it — if you do, Cyndaquil will be likely to shoot flames out of its back! Cyndaquil is a truly timid Pokémon but if it's provoked, or attacked it will flare up its back to protect itself.

#156 QUILAVA™

Quilava is the second evolutionary stage of Cyndaquil. This Fire Pokémon is totally covered with non-flammable fur so it can withstand ANY flame attack! If you find yourself facing the backside of one of these fiery Pokémon, watch out 'cause that usually means it's about to launch a huge flame attack on its opponent!

How to say it:
Qwi-LAVA

Type: Fire

Height: 2' 11"

Weight: 42 lbs.

Attacks:
EMBER, QUICK
ATTACK, FLAME WHEEL

Evolution:
Quilava evolves
into Typhlosion.

#157 TYPHLOSION™
VOLCANO Pokémon

How to say it:
Tie-FLOW-sion

Type: Fire

Height: 5' 07"

Weight: 175 lbs.

Attacks:
FLAME WHEEL, SWIFT, FLAMETHROWER

Evolution:
Typhlosion is the evolved form of Cyndaquil and Quilava.

This is the final evolutionary stage of Cyndaquil and Quilava. This super-hot Pokémon has some devastating attacks, but it has one super-secret move — it rubs its blazing fur together to cause mega-huge explosions! Also, be careful not to make it mad, for when Typhlosion's rage peaks, its fur gets so hot that anything that touches it will instantly go up in flames!

#158 TOTODILE™
BIG JAW Pokémon

This little Water Pokémon is the last of the three starter Pokémon that new trainers may get to begin their Johto adventure. This rough and tumble Pokémon is a great fighter and its super-strong jaws are capable of crushing most anything. It is an excitable Pokémon and it won't hesitate to take a bite out of anything that moves. Even its trainers must be careful!

How to say it:
TOT-ō-dile

Type: Water

Height: 2' 00"

Weight: 21 lbs.

Attacks:
SCRATCH, LEER, RAGE, WATER GUN

Evolution:
Totodile evolves into Croconaw.

Pokédex Pick:
In Ash's first adventure in Johto, he has to rescue a stolen Totodile from the nefarious Team Rocket. Ash and the gang all think the little Water Pokémon is very cute — and Ash eventually captures one!

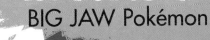

#159 CROCONAW™
BIG JAW Pokémon

How to say it:
CROCK-ō-naw

Type: Water

Height: 3' 07"

Weight: 55 lbs.

Attacks:
RAGE, WATER GUN,
BITE, SCARY FACE

Evolution:
Croconaw evolves
into Feraligatr.

Croconaw is the second evolutionary stage for Totodile. This Pokémon has a monstrous jaw that it uses very well in battle! When it clamps down on an opponent, it may lose one of its 48 fangs in the struggle — but not to worry, it will always grow another fang if it loses any!

#160 FERALIGATR™
BIG JAW Pokémon

This Pokémon is the final evolutionary form of Totodile and Croconaw. Feraligatr is so massive that it has a hard time supporting its weight out of the water, so it will get down on all fours to maneuver in the battlefield. In addition to some great water attacks, Feraligatr can bite with its awesomely powerful jaws to disable an opponent — and when it clamps down, it shakes its head to tear up its victim.

How to say it:
Fer-AL-i-gay-ter

Type: Water

Height: 7' 7"

Weight: 196 lbs.

Attacks:
BITE, SCARY FACE,
SLASH, SCREECH,
HYDRO PUMP

Evolution:
Feraligatr is the
evolved form of
Totodile and Croconaw.

#161 SENTRET

SCOUT Pokémon

How to say it:
SEN-trit

Type: Normal

Height: 2' 07"

Weight: 13 lbs.

Attacks:
TACKLE, DEFENSE
CURL, QUICK ATTACK

Evolution:
Sentret evolves
into Furret.

This Pokémon is very cautious and wary of danger. It has an extremely useful tail that it uses for a host of different purposes. For example, it will stand up straight on its tail to survey its surroundings and look for any impending danger on the horizon. If a Sentret spots any oncoming danger, it will cry out loudly to alert the rest of its kind.

#162 FURRET

LONG BODY Pokémon

Furret is the final evolved form of Sentret. When evolved its body is so long that there is no telling where the body ends and the tail begins! The nest that a Furret makes for itself is created specifically for its long body and it is nearly impossible for any other Pokémon to enter it. Furret may look unimposing, but despite its short, stubby legs, it is quick at hunting Rattata!

How to say it:
FUR-et

Type: Normal

Height: 5' 11"

Weight: 72 lbs.

Attacks:
FURY SWIPES, SLAM,
REST, AMNESIA

Evolution:
Furret is the
evolved form
of Sentret.

#163 HOOTHOOT™
OWL Pokémon

How to say it:
HOOT-hoot

Type: Normal/ Flying

Height: 2' 04"

Weight: 47 lbs.

Attacks:
TACKLE, GROWL,
FORESIGHT, PECK

Evolution:
Hoothoot evolves
into Noctowl.

This nocturnal (it only comes out at night!) Pokémon is a great companion for those dark and stormy nights. It has a perfect sense of time! Whatever happens to it, it keeps rhythm by precisely tilting its head in time. A curious creature, Hoothoot always stands on one foot and it changes feet so fast that the movement can rarely be seen.

#164 NOCTOWL™
OWL Pokémon

This majestic looking Pokémon is the second and final evolution of the owl-like Pokémon Hoothoot. Noctowl's eyes are specially adapted for nighttime viewing and watching! They concentrate even the most faint and distant light and are able to see everything perfectly in the dark. When a Noctowl needs to think, it will rotate its head 180 degrees to sharpen its intellectual power.

How to say it:
NOCT-owl

Type: Normal/ Flying

Height: 5' 03"

Weight: 90 lbs.

Attacks:
REFLECT, TAKE
DOWN, CONFUSION

Evolution:
Noctowl
is the
evolved
form of
Hoothoot.

Pokédex Pick:
Ash has a very peculiar Noctowl in his Pokémon collection. It has an exceedingly rare feather coloration!

#165 LEDYBA™
FIVE STAR Pokémon

How to say it:
LAY-dee-bah

Type: Bug/Flying

Height: 3' 03"

Weight: 24 lbs.

Attacks:
TACKLE,
SUPERSONIC,
COMET PUNCH

Evolution:
Ledyba evolves
into Ledian.

This Pokémon is a scaredy-bug! If one encounters a solitary Ledyba, it will be so afraid that it will not move, but if one encounters a group of Ledyba, they will be active and rambunctious. These Pokémon do not like winter and when the weather begins to turn cold, Ledyba from all over will gather together to huddle and keep warm!

#166 LEDIAN™
FIVE STAR Pokémon

This Pokémon is the second and final evolutionary form of Ledyba. The star patterns on the backs of these bug Pokémon grow larger or smaller depending on the number of stars in the night sky. Also, when those nighttime stars flicker in the sky, Ledian flutter about, scattering a glowing powder.

How to say it:
LAY-dee-an

Type: Bug/Flying

Height: 4' 07"

Weight: 78 lbs.

Attacks:
LIGHT SCREEN, BATON
PASS, COMET PUNCH,
SWIFT, SUBMISSION

Evolution:
Ledian is the
evolved form
of Ledyba.

#167 SPINARAK™
STRING SPIT Pokémon

How to say it:
SPIN-a-rack

Type: Bug/ Poison

Height: 1' 08"

Weight: 19 lbs.

Attacks:
POISON STING,
STRING SHOT, SCARY
FACE, CONSTRICT,
NIGHT SHADE

Evolution:
Spinarak evolves
into Ariados.

These spiderlike Pokémon are very patient. They spin a web using fine — but durable — thread and then it waits patiently, sometimes in the same position for days on end, for some unsuspecting prey to get caught!

Pokédex Pick:
Not only are the Growlithe employed by the numerous Officer Jennys in the Pokémon world, but Spinarak as well! Spinarak are the Pokémon of choice for a specific Johto police force.

#168 ARIADOS™
LONG LEG Pokémon

Ariados is the second and final evolutionary stage for Spinarak. A single strand of special webbing is endlessly spun out of its rear. This web leads back to the nest of the Ariados. Strangely, The Ariados does not only spin webbing out of its rear, but from its mouth as well. It is hard to tell which end is which.

How to say it:
ARE-ee-a-dos

Type: Bug/ Poison

Height: 3' 07"

Weight: 74 lbs.

Attacks:
LEECH LIFE, FURY
SWIPES, SPIDER WEB,
SCREECH, PSYCHIC

Evolution:
Ariados is the
evolved form
of Spinarak.

How to say it:
CROW–bat

Type:
Poison/ Flying

Height:
5' 11"

Weight:
165 lbs.

Attacks:
SCREECH, LEECH LIFE, SUPERSONIC, CONFUSE RAY

Evolution:
Crobat is the evolved form of Zubat and Goldbat.

This is the final evolutionary stage of Zubat and Golbat. The development of wings on this Pokémon's legs enables it to fly at very fast speeds, but also makes it tough for the Crobat to stop and rest. The two sets of wings of the Crobat allow this creature to fly so silently through the night that it may not be noticed even when it is nearby!

#170 CHINCHOU™
ANGLER Pokémon

How to say it:
CHIN-chow

Type: Water/ Electric

Height: 1' 08"

Weight: 26 lbs.

Attacks:
BUBBLE, THUNDER WAVE, SUPERSONIC, FLAIL, WATER GUN, SPARK

Evolution:
Chinchou evolves into Lanturn.

Found in the depths of the oceans, this Pokémon can only communicate by means of its constantly flashing lights. Upon further investigation, Chinchou shoots positive and negative electricity between the tips of its two antennae to zap its enemies.

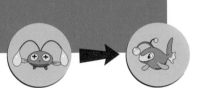

#171 LANTURN™
LIGHT Pokémon

Lanturn is the second and final evolutionary stage of Chinchou. This Water Electric Pokémon blinds its prey with intense bursts of light, then swallows the immobilized prey in a single gulp! It is also said that the light the Lanturn emits is so bright that it can illuminate the sea's surface from a depth of three miles!

How to say it:
LAN-turn

Type: Water/ Electric

Height: 3' 11"

Weight: 50 lbs.

Attacks:
SPARK, CONFUSE RAY, TAKE DOWN, HYDRO PUMP

Evolution:
Chinchou is the evolved form of Lanturn.

#172 PICHU™
MOUSE Pokémon

How to say it:
PEE-chew

Type:
Electric

Height:
1' 00"

Weight:
4 lbs.

Attacks:
THUNDERSHOCK,
CHARM, TAIL WHIP,
THUNDER WAVE,
SWEET KISS

Evolution:
Pichu evolves
into Pikachu.

This little electric mouse is the first evolutionary stage of Pikachu and Raichu. Despite its small stature, Pichu can zap even humans! Since it is so young, it is not very skilled at storing electricity so it may send out a stray jolt or two when amused or startled!

Pokédex Pick:

If you think Pikachu is cute, wait until you get a load if its preevolutionary form, Pichu! Pikachu meets up with two of these adorable little fellows in the third Pokémon movie.

35

#173 CLEFFA™
STARSHAPE Pokémon

How to say it:
CLEFF–ah

Type: Normal

Height: 1' 00"

Weight: 7 lbs.

Attacks:
POUND, CHARM, ENCORE, SING, SWEET KISS

Evolution:
Cleffa evolves into Clefairy.

Cleffa is the first evolutionary stage of Clefairy and Clefable. Like its evolutionary family, Cleffa's unusual starlike shape leads people to believe that it came here on a meteor! Mysteriously, when numerous meteors illuminate the night sky, sightings of Cleffa strangely increase.

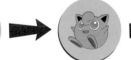

#174 IGGLYBUFF™
BALLOON Pokémon

This balloonlike Pokémon is the first evolutionary stage of Jigglypuff and Wigglytuff. The little Pokémon has a super-soft, extremely flexible and elastic body, and if it starts to roll, it will bounce all over the place and be impossible to stop!

How to say it:
IGG-lee-buff

Type: Normal

Height: 1' 00"

Weight: 2 lbs.

Attacks:
SING, CHARM, DEFENSE CURL, POUND, SWEET KISS

Evolution:
Igglybuff evolves into Jigglypuff.

#175 TOGEPI™
SPIKE BALL Pokémon

How to say it:
TOE-geh-pee

Type: **Normal**

Height: **1' 00"**

Weight: **3 lbs.**

Attacks:
CHARM, METRONOME, SWEET KISS, ENCORE, SAFEGUARD

Evolution:
Togepi evolves into Togetic.

A proverb claims that happiness will come to anyone who can make a sleeping Togepi stand up. The shell of the small Pokémon seems to be filled with joy — it is rumored that the Togepi will share good luck when treated kindly.

#176 TOGETIC™
HAPPINESS Pokémon

This is the final evolutionary stage of Togepi. This Pokémon is mysterious — it is said that a Togetic will appear before kindhearted, caring people and shower them with happiness. If not surrounded by kind people, the Togetic will grow dispirited. One more amazing characteristic of this Pokémon is that it can float in mid-air without moving its wings!

How to say it:
TOE- geh-tick

Type: **Normal/ Flying**

Height: **2' 00"**

Weight: **7 lbs.**

Attacks:
ENCORE, SAFEGUARD, DOUBLE-EDGE

Evolution:
Togetic is the evolved form of Togepi.

#177 NATU™
LITTLE BIRD Pokémon

How to say it:
NAH-too

Type: Psychic/ Flying

Height: 0' 08"

Weight: 4 lbs.

Attacks:
PECK, LEER, NIGHT
SHADE, TELEPORT

Evolution:
Natu evolves
into Xatu.

This little bird Pokémon's wings are not fully grown so it must hop around on the ground to forage for food. On rare occasions, it may be able to hop onto branches to peck at the small growth. An odd fact about Natu is that they are always staring at something. What they're staring at, we'll never know.

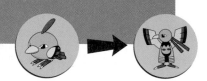

#178 XATU™
MYSTIC Pokémon

There is a legend in South America, told from generation to generation that the eyes of the Xatu are very special. The right eye of the Xatu sees into the future while its left eye views the past. This is the rumored reason why it stands so still and quiet.

How to say it:
ZAH-too

Type: Psychic/ Flying

Height: 4' 11"

Weight: 33 lbs.

Attacks:
FUTURE SIGHT,
CONFUSE RAY, PSYHIC

Evolution:
Xatu is the
evolved form
of Natu.

#179 MAREEP™
WOOL Pokémon

The fleece of this electric sheep is incredible! It is always growing — in the summer, the fleece is fully shed, but it grows back in one week! If some static electricity builds up in its body, its amazing fleece will double in volume. Touching the Mareep will shock you!

How to say it:
Ma-REEP

Type:
Electric

Height:
2' 00"

Weight:
17 lbs.

Attacks:
TACKLE, GROWL, THUNDERSHOCK

Evolution:
Mareep evolves into Flaaffy.

#180 FLAAFFY™
WOOL Pokémon

How to say it:
FLAAH-fee

Type: Electric

Height: 2' 07"

Weight: 29 lbs.

Attacks:
THUNDER WAVE,
COTTON SPORE

Evolution:
Flaaffy evolves
into Ampharos.

Flaaffy is the second evolutionary stage of Mareep. This evolved Electric Pokémon's fluffy fleece easily stores electricity and its rubbery skin keeps it from being electrocuted. As a direct result of storing too much electricity, Flaaffy have developed patches of skin where even downy wool won't grow.

#181 AMPHAROS™
LIGHT Pokémon

This Pokémon is the third and final evolutionary stage of Mareep and Flaaffy. The bright light on the tip of its tail can be seen from miles around. It has been treasured since ancient times as a beacon of light for those who are lost.

How to say it:
AM-fah-ross

Type: Electric

Height: 4' 07"

Weight: 136 lbs.

Attacks:
LIGHT SCREEN,
THUNDER

Evolution:
Ampharos is the
evolved form of
Mareep and Flaaffy.

How to say it:
Bell-AWE-sum

Type:
Grass

Height:
1' 04"

Weight:
13 lbs.

Attacks:
ABSORB, SWEET SCENT, STUN SPORE, PETAL DANCE, SOLARBEAM

Evolution:
Bellossom is one of the two evolved forms of Gloom.

These beautiful Flower Pokémon are extremely plentiful in the tropics where they gather at times and appear to dance. When it dances, its petals rub together and make a pleasant ringing sound. It has been rumored that the dance of the Bellossom is a ritual to summon the sun!

#183 MARILL™
AQUAMOUSE Pokémon

How to say it:
MARE-ill

Type:
Water

Height:
1' 04"

Weight:
19 lbs.

Attacks:
TACKLE, DEFENSE CURL, TAIL WHIP, WATER GUN, ROLLOUT

Evolution:
Marill evolves into Azumarill.

The ball on the end of this small Pokémon's tail is filled with an oil that is lighter than water. The ball serves as a buoy or floatation device that keeps the Marill from drowning, even if it's swimming in a vicious current.

#184 AZUMARILL™
AQUARABBIT Pokémon

Azumarill is the second and final evolutionary stage of Marill. When this Pokémon plays in the water, it rolls up its super-long ears to prevent any water from getting inside of them. Also, by keeping very still and listening closely, it can tell what Pokémon are in any type of moving water — even wild, fast-moving rivers.

How to say it:
Ah-ZOO-mare-ill

Type:
Water

Height:
2' 07"

Weight:
63 lbs.

Attacks:
TAIL WHIP, WATER GUN, DOUBLE-EDGE, BUBBLE BEAM

Evolution:
Azumarill is the evolved form of Marill.

#185 SUDOWOODO™
IMITATION Pokémon

How to say it:
Sood-Ō-wood-Ō

Type: Rock

Height: 3' 11"

Weight: 84 lbs.

Attacks:
ROCK THROW, MIMIC, FLAIL, LOW KICK, ROCK SIDE, FAINT ATTACK, SLAM

Evolution:
Sudowoodo does not evolve.

This Pokémon is a mystery. Although it disguises itself and often pretends to be a tree to avoid detection and attack, its composition appears to be closer to a rock than a plant. That being said, Sudowoodo hate water (like Rock Pokémon should), so they will disappear if it starts raining.

#186 POLITOED™
FROG Pokémon

How to say it:
PAUL-ee-toad

Type: Water

Height: 3' 07"

Weight: 75 lbs.

Attacks:
WATER GUN, HYPNOSIS, DOUBLE SLAP, PERISH SONG, SWAGGER

Evolution:
Politoed is one of the two evolved forms of Poliwhirl.

If some Poliwag and Poliwhirl hear the echoing cry of the Politoed, they respond by gathering together from far and wide. In addition to being an evolutionary enigma, whenever three or more of these Pokémon get together, they sing in a loud voice that sounds like bellowing.

These super-light creatures must grip the ground tightly with their small feet to keep from being blown away by the wind. Another way these little Pokémon save themselves from the blustery gales is huddling in groups. Although it may not seem like it, these tiny Pokémon do enjoy gentle breezes.

How to say it:
HOP-pip

Type:
Grass/ Flying

Height:
1' 04"

Weight:
1 lbs.

Attacks:
SPLASH, SYNTHESIS, TAIL WHIP, TACKLE, POISON POWDER, STUN SPORE

Evolution:
Hoppip evolves into Skiploom.

Pokédex Pick:
The small pink "cottonweed" Hoppip was once used to predict the weather!

#188 SKIPLOOM™
COTTONWEED Pokémon

How to say it:
SKIP-ploom

Type: Grass/ Flying

Height: 2' 00"

Weight: 2 lbs.

Attacks:
POISON POWDER,
STUN SPORE, SLEEP
POWDER, LEECH SEED,
COTTON SPORE

Evolution:
Skiploom evolves
into Jumpluff.

This is the second evolutionary stage of Hoppip. This flowery creature spreads its petals to absorb the sunlight and it floats on the air to get closer to the sun itself. The large bloom on its head opens and closes as the temperature around it fluctuates up and down.

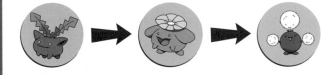

#189 JUMPLUFF™
COTTONWEED Pokémon

Jumpluff is the third and final evolutionary form of Hoppip and Skiploom. This floating Pokémon drifts and catches seasonal winds to spread its cotton-like spores all over the world to make more offspring.

How to say it:
JUMP-pluff

Type: Grass/ Flying

Height: 2' 07"

Weight: 7 lbs.

Attacks:
STUN SPORE, SLEEP
POWDER, LEECH SEED,
COTTON SPORE,
MEGA DRAIN

Evolution:
Jumpluff is the
evolved form of
Hoppip and Skiploom.

#190 AIPOM™
LONG TAIL Pokémon

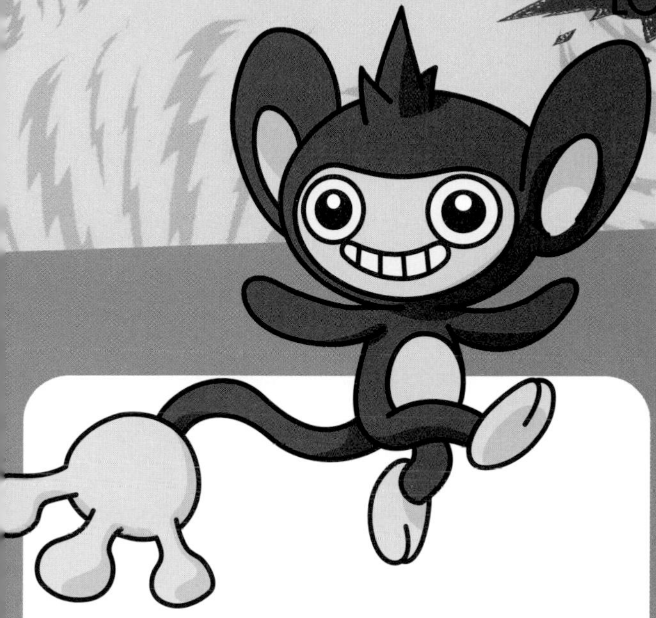

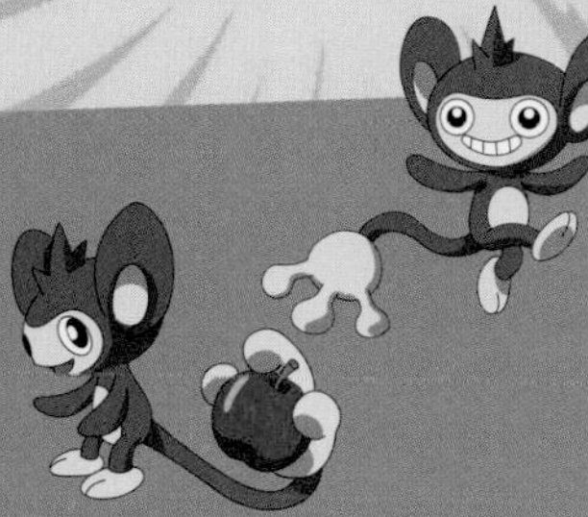

How to say it:
Ā-pom

Type:
Normal

Height:
2' 07"

Weight:
25 lbs.

Attacks:
SAND ATTACK, BATON PASS, FURY SWIPES, SWIFT, AGILITY

Evolution:
Aipom does not evolve.

This Pokémon lives in the tops of very tall trees. When leaping from branch to branch, it deftly uses its amazing tail for balance. The Aipom's tail is so powerful that it can use it to grab a tree branch and hold itself up in the air!

Pokédex Pick:
In the movie *Spell of the Unown*, Aipom is one of the six Pokémon that trainer Lisa uses in her battle against Ash.

#191 SUNKERN
SEED Pokémon

How to say it:
SUN-kern

Type: Grass

Height: 0' 01"

Weight: 4 lbs.

Attacks:
ABSORB, GROWTH, MEGA DRAIN, SUNNY DAY, SYNTHESIS, GIGA DRAIN

Evolution:
Sunkern evolves into Sunflora.

This Sunkern Pokémon lives solely by drinking the dewdrops that accumulate under the leaves of plants. Sunkern may drop out of the sky unexpectedly, and if attacked by any predators, it will violently shake its leaves.

This is the second and final evolved form of Sunkern. In the daytime, this Pokémon rushes about in a hectic manner, for it converts the sun's rays into energy. When the sun sets though, the Sunflora comes to a complete stop, closes its petals, and becomes perfectly still until sunrise.

#192 SUNFLORA
SUN Pokémon

How to say it:
Sun-FLOOR-uh

Type: Grass

Height: 2' 07"

Weight: 19 lbs.

Attacks:
POUND, RAZOR LEAF, SUNNY DAY, PETAL DANCE, SOLARBEAM

Evolution:
Sunflora is the evolved form of Sunkern.

Pokédex Pick:
Team Rocket once used a set of mirrors to distract Sunflora in order to pilfer a year's supply of Ramen Noodles!

#200 Misdreavus™
#207 Gligar™
#214 Heracross™
#221 Piloswine™

#199 Slowking™
#206 Dunsparce™
#213 Shuckle™
#220 Swinub™

#198 Murkrow™
#205 Forretress™
#212 Scizor™
#219 Magcargo™

#197 Umbreon™
#204 Pineco™
#211 Qwilfish™
#218 Slugma™

#196 Espeon™
#203 Girafarig™
#210 Granbull™
#217 Ursaring™

#195 Quagsire™
#202 Wobbuffet™
#209 Snubbull™
#216 Teddiursa™

#194 Wooper™
#201 Unown™
#208 Steelix™
#215 Sneasel™

#222 Corsola™ #223 Remoraid™ #224 Octillery™ #225 Delibird™ #226 Mantine™ #227 Skarmory™ #228 Houndour™

#229 Houndoom™ #230 Kingdra™ #231 Phanpy™ #232 Donphan™ #233 Porygon2™ #234 Stantler™ #235 Smeargle™

#236 Tyrogue™ #237 Hitmontop™ #238 Smoochum™ #239 Elekid™ #240 Magby™ #241 Miltank™ #242 Blissey™

#243 Raikou™ #244 Entei™ #245 Suicune™ #246 Larvitar™ #247 Pupitar™ #248 Tyranitar™ #249 Lugia™ #250 Ho-oh™

How to say it:
YAN-mah

Type:
Bug/ Flying

Height:
3' 11"

Weight:
84 lbs.

Attacks:
FORESIGHT, QUICK ATTACK, DOUBLE TEAM, SONICBOOM, SUPERSONIC, SWIFT

Evolution:
Yanma does not evolve.

Yanma's large eyes can scan 360 degrees! It can look in all directions to seek out smaller insects as its prey. If it flaps its clear wings really, really fast, it can generate shock waves that can shatter windows in the area.

#194 WOOPER™

WATER FISH Pokémon

How to say it:
WŌŌ-per

Type:
Water/ Ground

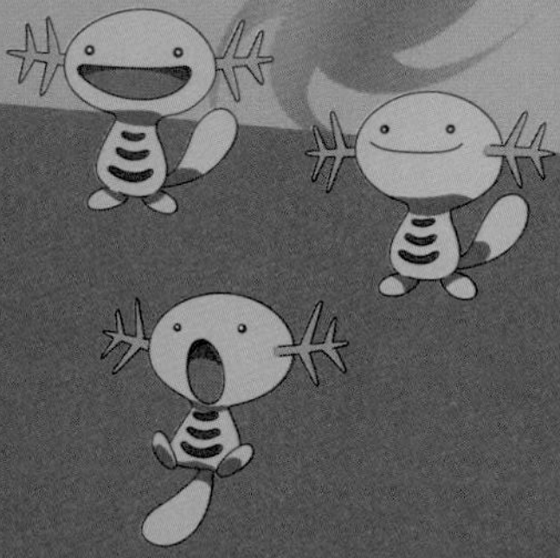

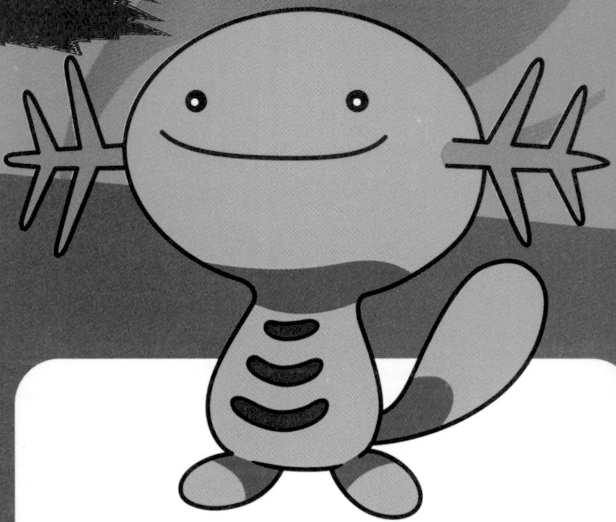

Height:
1' 04"

Weight:
19 lbs.

Attacks:
WATER GUN, TAIL WHIP, SLAM, AMNESIA

Evolution:
Wooper evolves into Quagsire.

When this Pokémon walks around on dry land, it coats its body with a slimy, poisonous film to protect itself. Wooper usually live in cold water, but they will leave the water to search for food when the outside temperature gets cold enough.

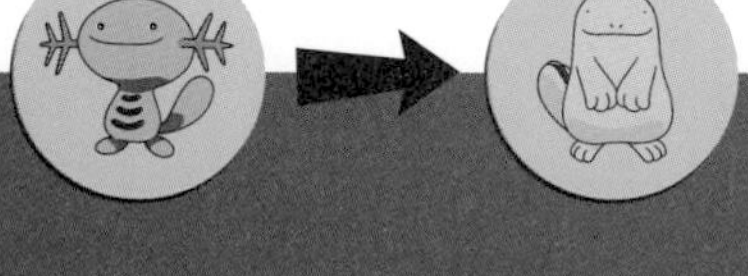

Quagsire is the second and final evolutionary form of Wooper. This carefree Pokémon has an easy-going nature, and due to its relaxed attitude, it often bumps its head on boulders and boat hulls as it swims. It is rumored that Quagsire like round objects.

How to say it:
QUĂG-sire

Type:
Water/ Ground

Height:
4' 07"

Weight:
165 lbs.

Attacks:
EARTHQUAKE, RAIN DANCE, MIST, HAZE, WATER GUN, SLAM, AMNESIA

Evolution:
Quagsire is the evolved form of Wooper.

Pokédex Pick:
Quagsire have a very odd liking for things that are round! Herds of Quagsire collect round objects and then, mysteriously, they hurl them at the moon! The object that got "closest" to the moon — the GS Ball!

51

#196 ESPEON™
SUN Pokémon

How to say it:
ESS-pee-on

Type:
Psychic

Height:
2' 11"

Weight:
58 lbs.

Attacks:
TACKLE, TAIL WHIP,
SAND ATTACK,
CONFUSION

Evolution:
Espeon is an
evolved form
of Eevee.

Espeon is the fourth of
the five different evolutions
of Eevee, the first three
being Vaporeon, Jolteon,
and Flareon. By reading air
currents with the fine hair
that covers its body, Espeon
can predict things such
as the weather or its
foe's next move.

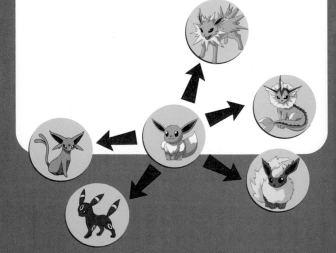

Umbreon is the fifth of the five evolutionary forms of the Pokémon Eevee. When darkness falls, the rings on the body of an Umbreon begin to glow, striking fear into he hearts of anyone nearby. When agitated, this Dark Pokémon protects itself by spraying poisonous sweat from its pores!

How to say it:
UMM-bree-on

Type:
Dark

Height:
3' 03"

Weight:
60 lbs.

Attacks:
PURSUIT, CONFUSE RAY, FAINT ATTACK, MEAN LOOK, SCREECH, MOONLIGHT

Evolution:
Umbreon is an evolved form of Eevee.

Pokédex Pick:

Eevee's got two new evolutions! During one of Ash's adventures within the Johto countryside, he meets up with Gary again. This time, though, Ash faces off against Gary's newly evolved Umbreon! Gary and Ash eventually have to team to save the day.

#198 MURKROW™

How to say it:
MUR–krow

Type:
Dark/ Flying

Height:
1' 08"

Weight:
5 lbs.

Attacks:
PECK, PURSUIT, HAZE,
NIGHT SHADE, FAINT
ATTACK, MEAN LOOK

Evolution:
Murkrow does
not evolve.

There is a rumor that if a Murkrow is being chased, it will lure its attacker onto a dark mountain trail where the foe will get lost! This Pokémon is feared and hated by many people, and it is believed to bring misfortune to all who look upon one at night.

This Pokémon is another evolutionary form of Slowpoke. Instead of the Shellder clamping onto its tail, it clamps onto the Slowpoke's head. When its head is bitten, toxins enter the Slowpoke's head and extraordinary powers are unlocked! This Pokémon has incredible intellect and intuition. Whatever the situation, it remains calm and collected.

How to say it:
SLOW-king

Type:
Water/ Psychic

Height:
6' 07"

Weight:
175 lbs.

Attacks:
CURSE, WATER GUN, CONFUSION, DISABLE, HEADBUTT, SWAGGER, PSYCHIC

Evolution:
Slowking is an evolved form of Slowpoke.

Pokédex Pick:
The amazing Slowking was one of the major characters in Pokémon The Movie 2000: The Power of One. If it wasn't for this intelligent Pokémon, Ash and the gang would never have succeeded in their endeavor to save the world.

#200 MISDREAVUS™
SCREECH Pokémon

How to say it:
MISS-dreav-us

Type:
Ghost

Height:
2' 04"

Weight:
2 lbs.

Attacks:
PSYWAVE, SPITE,
CONFUSE RAY, MEAN
LOOK, PSYBEAM, PAIN
SPLIT, PERISH SONG

Evolution:
Misdreavus does
not evolve.

This ghostly Pokémon likes to bite and yank people's hair from behind without warning, just to see the shocked expressions on their terrified faces! It also likes playing mischievous tricks such as howling and screaming to startle innocent people at night.

#201 UNOWN™
SYMBOL Pokémon

How to say it:
UN-nown

Type:
Psychic

Height:
1' 08"

Weight:
11 lbs.

Attacks:
HIDDEN POWER

Evolution:
**Unown does
not evolve.**

Its flat, thin body is always stuck fast to walls. Its shape is also reminiscent of ancient hieroglyphs. The shapes and the hieroglyphs are alleged to be somehow connected.

Pokédex Pick:

The mysterious Pokémon known as Unown has 26 different shapes. They are hieroglyphic representations of the alphabet!

#202 WOBBUFFET™
PATIENT Pokémon

How to say it:
WAH-buff-ett

Type: Psychic

Height: 4' 03"

Weight: 63 lbs.

Attacks:
COUNTER, MIRROR COAT, DESTINY BOND

Evolution:
Wobbuffet does not evolve.

To keep its pitch-black tail hidden, this Pokémon chooses to live quietly in the darkness, for it hates the light. It is never the first one to attack, but if it is attacked, it inflates its body to pump up its counterstrike!

Pokédex Pick:
In a Pokémon Swap Meet Jessie loses her Lickitung for a Psyduckesque, non-descript Wobbuffet. What a bummer!

Pokédex Pick:
Girafarig's "Future Sight" allows the Pokémon to launch an attack and then have the attack hit the opponent a few moments into the future! This amazing ability was used against Pikachu during a battle between Ash and a young female trainer during his Johto adventure. Ash never saw it coming!

#203 GIRAFARIG™
LONG NECK Pokémon

This Pokémon's tail contains a small brain. If it smells something alluring, it may reach out of its own accord and bite! So beware! If you get too close to Girafarig, it may react to your scent and bite!

How to say it:
Jir-AFF-uh-rig

Type: Normal/ Psychic

Height: 4' 11"

Weight: 91 lbs.

Attacks:
CONFUSION, STOMP, GROWL, TACKLE

Evolution:
Girafarig does not evolve.

#204 PINECO™
BAGWORM Pokémon

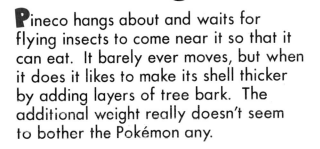

How to say it:
PINE-kō

Type: Bug

Height: 2' 00"

Weight: 16 lbs.

Attacks:
SELF DESTRUCT, TAKE DOWN, RAPID SPIN, BIDE

Evolution:
Pineco evolves into Forretress.

Pineco hangs about and waits for flying insects to come near it so that it can eat. It barely ever moves, but when it does it likes to make its shell thicker by adding layers of tree bark. The additional weight really doesn't seem to bother the Pokémon any.

#205 FORRETRESS™
BAGWORM Pokémon

Forretress is the second and final evolutionary form of Pineco. This Pokémon's entire body is shielded by a steel-hard shell. What lurks inside the armor is a total mystery! Forretress remain immovably rooted to their trees and scatter pieces of their super-hard shell to drive away any enemies.

How to say it:
FOUR-ett-tress

Type: Bug/ Steel

Height: 3' 11"

Weight: 277 lbs.

Attacks:
EXPLOSION, SPIKES, SUBMISSION, DOUBLE-EDGE

Evolution:
Forretress is the evolved form of Pineco.

#206 DUNSPARCE
LAND SNAKE Pokémon

How to say it:
DUNN-sparce

Type: Normal

Height: 4' 11"

Weight: 31 lbs.

Attacks:
RAGE, DEFENSE CURL, GLARE, SPITE, PURSUIT, SCREECH, TAKE DOWN

Evolution:
Dunsparce does not evolve.

This Pokémon can just barely float above the ground using its wings, but if it's spotted by anyone or anything — look out! It escapes backwards by furiously boring into the ground with its tail.

Pokédex Pick:
A man dressed as a spider? A man dressed with a cape? In the Pokémon world, they have the superhero named Gligarman! This hero has taken on disguise of the batlike Pokémon Gligar to battle evil.

#207 GLIGAR
FLYSCORPIO Pokémon

This Pokémon usually clings to the sides of cliffs, and when it spots its prey, it spreads its wings and glides down to attack. The Gligar will fly straight at its target's face then clamp down on the startled victim to inject poison.

How to say it:
GLIE-ger

Type: Ground/ Flying

Height: 3' 07"

Weight: 143 lbs.

Attacks:
POISON STING, SAND THROW, BITE, SLASH, SCREECH, GUILLOTINE

Evolution:
Gligar does not evolve.

#208 STEELIX™
IRON SNAKE Pokémon

How to say it:
STEEL–icks

Type:
Steel/ Ground

Height:
30' 02"

Weight:
882 lbs.

Attacks:
BIND, ROCK THROW,
TACKLE, SCREECH

Evolution:
Steelix is the
evolved form
of Onix.

This is the second and final evolutionary stage of Onix. There is an old rumor that if an Onix lives for over one hundred years, its composition changes to become diamond-like. The body of a Steelix — so say scientists — has been compressed deep under the ground. As a result, it is even harder than a diamond.

#209 SNUBBULL™
FAIRY Pokémon

How to say it:
SNUB–bull

Type: Normal

Height: 2' 08"

Weight: 17 lbs.

Attacks:
SCARY FACE,
TAIL WHIP, CHARM,
BITE, LICK, ROAR

Evolution:
Snubbull evolves
into Granbull.

Although this Pokémon looks frightening, it actually has a very kind, affectionate, and playful nature. It is a very popular Pokémon among women!

Pokédex Pick:
Snubbull may look sweet, but they are a really tough Pokémon in a pinch. Even when Ash and the gang meet a seemingly pampered Pokémon — the Snubbull wants to "snub" the high life and be a real Pokémon.

#210 GRANBULL™
FAIRY Pokémon

This is the second and final evolutionary stage of Snubbull. Because its massive fangs are too heavy, it always keeps its head tilted down. However, its bite is very powerful! Granbull are actually very timid and easily spooked. If one of these bulldoglike Pokémon are attacked, it will flail to fend off its attacker.

How to say it:
GRAN–bull

Type: Normal

Height: 4' 07"

Weight: 107 lbs.

Attacks:
BITE, LICK, ROAR,
RAGE, TAKE DOWN

Evolution:
Granbull is the
evolved form
of Snubbull.

#211 QWILFISH
BALLOON Pokémon

How to say it:
QUILL-fish

Type: Water/ Poison

Height: 1' 08"

Weight: 9 lbs.

Attacks:
POISON STING,
MINIMIZE, WATER GUN,
PIN MISSILE, TAKE
DOWN, HYDRO PUMP

Evolution:
Qwilfish does
not evolve.

The small spikes covering this Pokémon's body "evolved" from scales. They inject a toxin that causes fainting. In order to fire its toxin, the Qwilfish must inflate its body by drinking over 2.6 gallons of water all at once!

Scizor is the second and final evolutionary stage of Scyther. The wings of the Scizor are not used for flying. The wings are flapped at super-high speeds to adjust its body temperature. The Scizor swings its eye-patterned pincers up to scare oncoming foes. This maneuver makes it look like the Scizor has three heads.

#212 SCIZOR
SCISSORS Pokémon

Pokédex Pick:
In the Johto Universe, there are new Pokémon that are new evolutions of old Pokémon. For example, the sleek Scizor is the final evolution of Scyther, and Kingdra is the final evolution of Horsea and Seadra!

How to say it:
SIE-zor

Type: Bug/ Steel

Height: 5' 11"

Weight: 260 lbs.

Attacks:
FOCUS ENERGY,
PURSUIT, FALSE
SWIPE, AGILITY,
METAL CLAW, SLASH,
SWORDS DANCE,
DOUBLE TEAM

Evolution:
Scizor is the evolved form of Scyther.

63

#213 SHUCKLE™
MOLD Pokémon

How to say it:
SHUK-ul

Type: Bug/ Rock

Height: 2' 00"

Weight: 45 lbs.

Attacks:
CONSTRICT, WITHDRAW, WRAP, ENCORE

Evolution:
Shuckle does not evolve.

This Pokémon has an odd habit of storing berries inside its shell. The berries that it stores in its vaselike shell decompose and become a gooey liquid! To avoid attacks, the Shuckle hides beneath rocks and remains completely still.

#214 HERACROSS™
SINGLEHORN Pokémon

This Pokémon is usually docile, but if it is disturbed while sipping honey, it chases off the intruder with its massive horn. When truly provoked to fight, this powerful Pokémon will thrust its two-pronged horn under its enemies' bellies, then lifts and throws them!

How to say it:
HAIR-a-cross

Type: Bug/ Fighting

Height: 4' 11"

Weight: 119 lbs.

Attacks:
HORN ATTACK, ENDURE, FURY ATTACK, COUNTER, TAKE DOWN, REVERSAL, MEGAHORN

Evolution:
Heracross does not evolve.

Pokédex Pick:
The first Pokémon that Ash catches on his Johto Journey is a Heracross.

#215 SNEASEL™
SHARP CLAW Pokémon

How to say it:
SNEE-zul

Type: Dark/ Ice

Height: 2' 11"

Weight: 62 lbs.

Attacks:
SCREECH, SCRATCH, LEER, QUICK ATTACK

Evolution:
Sneasel does not evolve.

A vicious Pokémon by nature, the Sneasel drives Pidgey from their nests, and feasts on the eggs that are left behind! The paws of a Sneasel conceal sharp claws. If attacked, it suddenly extends the claws and startles the enemy.

#216 TEDDIURSA™
LITTLEBEAR Pokémon

If this little bear Pokémon finds honey, the crescent mark on its body glows. It is perpetually licking its paws because they are always soaked with honey! A resourceful Pokémon, before food becomes scarce in the wintertime, its habit is to hoard food in many hidden locations.

How to say it:
Ted-eee-UR-sa

Type: Normal

Height: 2' 00"

Weight: 19 lbs.

Attacks:
LICK, FURY SWIPES, FAINT ATTACK, REST

Evolution:
Teddiursa evolves into Ursaring.

#217 URSARING™
HIBERNATE Pokémon

How to say it:
UR-sa-ring

Type:
Normal

Height:
5' 11"

Weight:
277 lbs.

Attacks:
SLASH, SNORE, THRASH

Evolution:
Ursaring is the evolved form of Teddiursa.

This Pokémon is the second and final evolutionary stage for Teddiursa. Although it is a good climber, Ursaring prefers to snap trees with its forelegs and eat fallen berries off the ground. The Ursaring have an amazing ability to distinguish any aroma. They can unfailingly find all food that is buried deep underground.

#218 SLUGMA™
LAVA Pokémon

How to say it:
SLUG-ma

Type: Fire

Height: 2' 04"

Weight: 77 lbs.

Attacks:
SMOG, EMBER,
ROCK THROW,
HARDEN, AMNESIA

Evolution:
Slugma evolves
into Magcargo.

A common sight in volcanic areas, the Slugma slowly slithers about in a constant search for warm areas. A fun fact is that the Slugma never sleep. It must always keep moving because if it is stopped, its magma body would cool and harden.

Magcargo is the second and final evolutionary stage for Slugma. The large shell on its back is just skin that has cooled and hardened. It breaks easily with just a slight touch. That same brittle shell will occasionally spout intense flames that circulate throughout its body.

#219 MAGCARGO™
LAVA Pokémon

How to say it:
Mug-CAR-go

Type: Fire/ Rock

Height: 2' 07"

Weight: 121 lbs.

Attacks:
FLAMETHROWER,
ROCK SLIDE, BODY
SLAM

Evolution:
Magcargo is the
evolved form
of Slugma.

#220 SWINUB
PIG Pokémon

How to say it:
SWINE-ub

Type: Ice/ Ground

Height: 1' 04"

Weight: 14 lbs.

Attacks:
TACKLE, POWDER SNOW, ENDURE, TAKE DOWN, MIST

Evolution:
Swinub evolves into Piloswine.

If this Pokémon smells something enticing, it dashes headlong off to find the source of the aroma. It will then rub its snout on the ground to find and dig up appetizing food. It sometimes even discovers hot springs!

#221 PILOSWINE
SWINE Pokémon

This Pokémon is the second and final evolutionary stage of Swinub. If this Pokémon charges at its enemy, the hairs on its back stand straight up. Because of these long hairs that cover its entire body, its sight is obstructed. This causes the very sound sensitive Piloswine to keep charging at its attacker repeatedly.

How to say it:
PILE-a-swine

Type: Ice/ Ground

Height: 3' 07"

Weight: 123 lbs.

Attacks:
FURY ATTACK, MIST, BLIZZARD

Evolution:
Piloswine is the evolved form of Swinub.

How to say it:
Course-ola

Type:
Water/ Rock

Height:
2' 00"

Weight:
11 lbs.

Attacks:
BUBBLE, RECOVER, BUBBLE BEAM, SPIKE CANNON, MIRROR COAT, ANCIENT POWER

Evolution:
Corsola does not evolve.

In a South Sea nation, the native people live in communities that are built on groups of these Pokémon! The Corsola continually sheds and grows. The tip of its head is prized as a treasure for its beauty.

#223 REMORAID™

JET Pokémon

How to say it:
REM-or-aid

Type: Water

Height: 2' 00"

Weight: 26 lbs.

Attacks:
WATER GUN, LOCK ON, PSYBEAM, AURORA BEAM, BUBBLE BEAM

Evolution:
Remoraid evolves into Octillery.

Using its dorsal fin as a suction cup, this small fishlike Pokémon cling to the undersides of Mantine to scavenge for leftover food! It's not completely dependent on Mantine. It has superb accuracy. The water it shoots out can strike even moving prey from more than 300 feet.

#224 OCTILLERY™

JET Pokémon

This Pokémon instinctively sneaks into rocky holes. If it gets sleepy, it will steal the nest of another Octillery. When looking for food, it will trap its enemies with its suction-cupped tentacles, then smash the captured prey with its rock-hard head.

How to say it:
Ock-TILL-uh-ree

Type: Water

Height: 2' 11"

Weight: 63 lbs.

Attacks:
OCTAZOOKA, FOCUS ENERGY, ICE BEAM, HYPER BEAM

Evolution:
Octillery is the evolved form of Remoraid.

#225 DELIBIRD™
DELIVERY Pokémon

How to say it:
DEL-i-bird

Type: Ice/ Flying

Height: 2' 00"

Weight: 35 lbs.

Attacks:
PRESENT

Evolution:
**Delibird does
not evolve.**

Its nests are at the edge of very sharp and high cliffs. It spends all day carrying food to its awaiting chicks. There are even tales of people who have been saved by the food that the Delibird carries.

Pokédex Pick:
Mantine has the honor of being the Johto Pokémon that weighs the most at a whopping 485 lbs!

#226 MANTINE™
KITE Pokémon

**Swimming freely in the open seas, the Mantine may fly out of the water and over the waves if it builds up enough speed. As it majestically swims through the ocean, it doesn't care if the tiny Remoraid attach to it for scavenging its leftovers.

How to say it:
MAN-tyne

Type: Water/ Flying

Height: 6' 11"

Weight: 485 lbs.

Attacks:
**BUBBLE, TAKE DOWN,
SUPERSONIC, WING,
BUBBLE BEAM, RAY
ATTACK, CONFUSE**

Evolution:
**Mantine does
not evolve.**

#227 SKARMORY™
ARMOR BIRD Pokémon

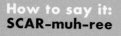

How to say it:
SCAR-muh-ree

Type:
Steel/ Flying

Height:
5' 07"

Weight:
111 lbs.

Attacks:
SAND ATTACK, SWIFT, AGILITY, FURY ATTACK, STEEL WING

Evolution:
Skarmory does not evolve.

Pokédex Pick:
It has been said that Skarmory — the Armor Bird Pokémon — is weak against Fire element Pokémon. Brock's Vulpix goes toe-to-wing against a female trainer's Skarmory to toughen the steely bird up!

After it makes its nest in bramble bushes, the wings of its newly born chicks grow hard from scratches by the thorny barbs of the brambles. Its sturdy, steely wings look heavy, but they are actually hollow and light, allowing it to fly freely in the sky.

#228 HOUNDOUR™
DARK Pokémon

How to say it:
Hownd-our

Type: Dark/ Fire

Height: 2' 00"

Weight: 24 lbs.

Attacks:
LEER, EMBER, ROAR, SMOG

Evolution:
Houndour evolves into Houndoom.

This fiery, dark, Pokémon uses different kinds of cries and barks for communicating with others of its kind and for pursuing prey. When cornering the prey, they check one another's locations using those special barks.

Pokédex Pick:
In the Johto universe, two new Pokémon elements have been discovered: Steel and Dark. A Dark type Pokémon was the cause of much thievery in one of Ash's adventures. It eventually turned out to be a pack of Houndour!

#229 HOUNDOOM™
DARK Pokémon

Houndoom is the second and final evolutionary stage of Houndour. Upon hearing its eerie howls, other Pokémon get the shivers and head straight back to their nests. It is rumored that if you are burned by the flames that the Houndoom shoots from its mouth, the pain will NEVER go away!

How to say it:
Hown-DOOM

Type: Dark/ Fire

Height: 4' 07"

Weight: 77 lbs.

Attacks:
FAINT ATTACK, FLAME THROWER, BITE, CRUNCH

Evolution:
Houndoom is the evolved form of Houndour.

#230 KINGDRA™
DRAGON Pokémon

How to say it:
KING–dra

Type:
Water/ Dragon

Height:
5' 11"

Weight:
335 lbs.

Attacks:
BUBBLE, LEER,
SMOKESCREEN,
WATER GUN

Evolution:
Kingdra is the
evolved form
of Horsea
and Seadra.

Kingdra is the third and final evolutionary stage of Horsea and Seadra. It sleeps and hides on the ocean floor in underwater caves to build up energy. It is alleged that it can create tornados and whirlpools when it wakes and yawns!

#231 PHANPY™
LONG NOSE Pokémon

How to say it:
FAN-pee

Type: Ground

Height: 1' 08"

Weight: 74 lbs.

Attacks:
**TACKLE, GROWL,
DEFENSE CURL, FLAIL,
TAKE DOWN**

Evolution:
**Phanpy evolves
into Donphan.**

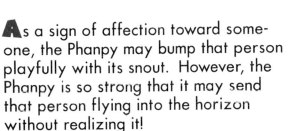

As a sign of affection toward someone, the Phanpy may bump that person playfully with its snout. However, the Phanpy is so strong that it may send that person flying into the horizon without realizing it!

Donphan is the final evolutionary stage of Phanpy. The longer and bigger its tusks, the higher its rank in the herd. These strong tusks take a very long time to grow. The Donphan has a very rugged hide and its Tackle Attack is strong enough to knock down a house!

#232 DONPHAN™
ARMOR Pokémon

How to say it:
DON-fan

Type: Ground

Height: 3' 07"

Weight: 265 lbs.

Attacks:
**HORN ATTACK,
GROWL, DEFENSE
CURL, ROLL OUT**

Evolution:
**Donphan is the
evolved form
of Phanpy.**

VIRTUAL Pokémon

How to say it:
PORE-ee-gone-too

Type:
Normal

Height:
2' 00"

Weight:
72 lbs.

Attacks:
**CANNON, TACKLE,
AGILITY, PSYBEAM,
CONVERSION**

Evolution:
**Porygon2 is
the evolved
form of Porygon.**

Porygon2 is the further researched and enhanced version of Porygon. This upgraded version of Porygon is designed for space exploration. It cannot fly — but sometimes it may exhibit motions that were not programmed.

#234 STANTLER
BIG HORN Pokémon

How to say it:
STANT-ler

Type: Normal

Height: 4' 07"

Weight: 157 lbs.

Attacks:
HYPNOSIS, STOMP, SAND-ATTACK, THRASH, CONFUSE RAY, TAKE DOWN

Evolution:
Stantler does not evolve.

Those who stare at its antlers will gradually lose control of their senses and be unable to stand. The curved antlers have the power to subtly change the flow of air in the area around itself and to create a strange space where reality itself becomes distorted!

#235 SMEARGLE
PAINTER Pokémon

Once this odd Pokémon becomes an adult, it gets a tendency to let its comrades plant footprints on its back! In order to do this, a special fluid oozes from the tip of its tail. It paints the fluid everywhere to mark its territory!

How to say it:
SMEAR-gull

Type: Normal

Height: 3' 11"

Weight: 128 lbs.

Attacks:
SKETCH

Evolution:
Smeargle does not evolve.

#236 TYROGUE™
SCUFFLE Pokémon

How to say it:
Ty-ROGE

Type:
Fighting

Height:
2' 04"

Weight:
46 lbs.

Attacks:
TACKLE

Evolution:
Tyrogue evolves into either Hitmonchan, Hitmontop, or Hitmonlee.

Even though it is small, this pugnacious Pokémon can't be ignored because it will slug any handy target without warning! It is always bursting with energy. To make itself stronger, it will keep on fighting even if it loses.

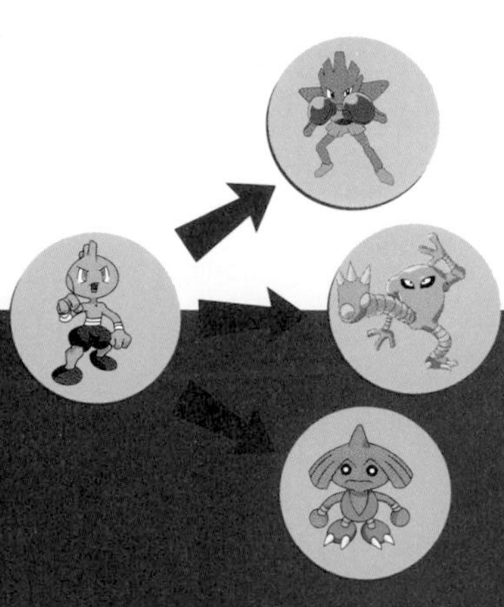

How to say it:
HIT-mon-top

Type:
Fighting

Height:
4' 07"

Weight:
106 lbs.

Attacks:
**ROLLING KICK,
FOCUS ENERGY,
RAPID SPIN**

Evolution:
**Hitmontop is one
of the three evolved
forms of Tyrogue.**

This Pokémon is another addition to the "Hitmon" family: Hitmonchan and Hitmonlee. It launches kicks while spinning. If it spins at high speeds, it may even bore its way into the ground! If you become enchanted by its smooth, elegant, dancelike kicks, you may get smacked upside your head!

Pokédex Pick:

Ash and the gang encounter a tenacious Hitmontop in an adventure that takes place within a fighting Pokémon Dojo (gym). Ash's Bulbasaur goes head-to-head with the spinning Pokémon… I wonder who comes out on top?

79

#238 SMOOCHUM™
KISS Pokémon

How to say it:
SMOOCH–um

Type:
Ice/ Psychic

Height:
1' 04"

Weight:
13 lbs.

Attacks:
POUND, LICK, SWEET KISS, POWDER SNOW, CONFUSION, SING

Evolution:
Smoochum evolves into Jynx.

Smoochum is the pre-evolutionary stage of Jynx. This sweet little Pokémon is always rocking its head slowly backwards and forwards as if it's trying to kiss someone. The lips are the most sensitive part of this Pokémon. It always uses its lips first to examine things.

#239 ELEKID™
ELECTRIC Pokémon

How to say it:
EL-eh-kid

Type: Electric

Height: 2' 00"

Weight: 52 lbs.

Attacks:
QUICK ATTACK, LEER,
THUNDERPUNCH

Evolution:
Elekid evolves
into Electabuzz.

Elekid is the pre-evolutionary stage of Electabuzz. Even in the most vicious storms, this little Electric Pokémon plays happily while the thunder rumbles violently in the sky. It will rotate its arms to generate electricity, but it gets tired easily, so it charges up only a little.

#240 MAGBY™
LIVE COAL Pokémon

Magby is the pre-evolutionary stage of Magmar. This fiery Pokémon is found primarily in volcanic craters. Its body temperature is over 1100 degrees, so don't get too close! Each time this Pokémon inhales and exhales, hot embers dribble out of its mouth and nostrils.

How to say it:
MAG-bee

Type: Fire

Height: 2' 04"

Weight: 47 lbs.

Attacks:
EMBER, SMOG,
FIRE PUNCH,
SMOKESCREEN,
SUNNY DAY

Evolution:
Magby evolves
into Magmar.

#241 MILTANK
MILK COW Pokémon

How to say it:
MIL-tank

Type:
Normal

Height:
3' 11"

Weight:
166 lbs.

Attacks:
STOMP, RECOVER, BIDE, ROLLOUT, BODY SLAM, HEAL BELL, MILK DRINK

Evolution:
Miltank does not evolve.

The milk of the Miltank is packed with nutrition, making it the ultimate beverage for the sick or weary. If this Pokémon has just had a baby, the milk it produces contains much more nutrition than usual.

Blissey is the second and final evolutionary form of Chansey. This Pokémon has a very compassionate nature, and if it sees a sick Pokémon, it will nurse the sufferer back to health. It is rumored that anyone who takes a bite out of Blissey's egg will become unfailingly pleasant to everyone!

How to say it:
BLISS-ee

Type:
Normal

Height:
4' 11"

Weight:
103 lbs.

Attacks:
POUND, SLAP, DOUBLE SLAP, MINIMIZE, SING, EGG BOMB, LIGHT SCREEN, SUBMISSION

Evolution:
Blissey is the evolved form of Chansey.

Pokédex Pick:
If you thought that Chansey was the only Pokémon that worked in the Pokémon Centers, you were wrong! Chansey's evolved form, Blissey, shares the nursing duties with Nurse Joy.

#243 RAIKOU™
THUNDER Pokémon

How to say it:
RIE-kō

Type:
Electric

Height:
6' 03"

Weight:
392 lbs.

Attacks:
THUNDERSHOCK,
ROAR, SPARK,
REFLECT, BITE,
THUNDER

Evolution:
Raikou does
not evolve.

This Pokémon races across the land while barking a cry that sounds like the crashing of thunder. The rain cloud that it carries on its back lets it fire massive thunderbolts at will. People say that this elusive Pokémon descended to Earth with lightning.

A very enigmatic Pokémon, it is rumored that one Entei is born every time a new volcano appears on the Earth. When this massive Pokémon barks, volcanoes erupt, and since it is unable to restrain its extreme powers it must constantly race about the land.

How to say it:
EN-tay

Type:
Fire

Height:
6' 11"

Weight:
437 lbs.

Attacks:
EMBER, ROAR, FIRE SPIN, STOMP, FLAMETHROWER, SWAGGER, FIRE BLAST

Evolution:
Entei does not evolve.

Pokédex Pick:
In the next Pokémon movie, Ash and the gang square off against one of the most elusive and powerful Pokémon ever — the mighty Entei.

#245 SUICUNE™
AURORA Pokémon

How to say it:
SWEE-koon

Type: Water

Height: 6' 07"

Weight: 412 lbs.

Attacks:
WATER GUN, ROAR,
GUST, BUBBLEBEAM,
MIST, MIRROR COAT,
HYDRO PUMP

Evolution:
Suicune does
not evolve.

It is whispered that this lithe, mysterious Pokémon is the reincarnation of the north winds. People say that Suicune has the magical ability to instantly purify filthy, murky, and polluted water.

#246 LARVITAR™
ROCK SKIN Pokémon

How to say it:
LAR-vay-tar

Type: Rock/ Ground

Height: 2' 00"

Weight: 159 lbs.

Attacks:
SAND STORM, ROCK SLIDE, THRASH

Evolution:
Larvitar evolves into Pupitar.

This strange creature is born deep underground and it can not emerge from its underground nest until it has entirely eaten the soil around it. After it has eaten an entire large mountain, it will fall asleep so that it can grow.

#247 PUPITAR™
HARD SHELL Pokémon

How to say it:
PUPE-i-tar

Type: Rock/ Ground

Height: 3' 11"

Weight: 335 lbs.

Attacks:
SCARY FACE, BITE, DIG, HYPER BEAM, CRUNCH

Evolution:
Pupitar evolves into Tyranitar.

Pupitar is the second evolutionary stage of Larvitar. Even sealed within its sheet-rock hard shell, this Pokémon can move freely. Hard, fast, and strong; it has enough power to thrash and topple a mountain!

How to say it:
Tie-RAN-i-tar

Type:
Rock/ Dark

Height:
6' 07"

Weight:
445 lbs.

Attacks:
SCARY FACE, BITE, DIG, HYPER BEAM, CRUNCH

Evolution:
Tyranitar is the evolved form of Larvitar and Pupitar.

Tyranitar is the third and final evolutionary form of Larvitar and Pupitar. Extremely strong, this Pokémon can change the very landscape! It has an insolent nature that makes it not care about others. Its body can't be harmed by any sort of attack, so it is very eager to make challenges against enemies.

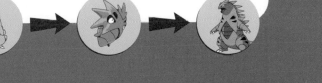

#249 LUGIA™
DIVING Pokémon

How to say it:
LU-gee-uh

Type:
Psychic/ Flying

Height:
17' 01"

Weight:
476 lbs.

Attacks:
AEROBLAST, GUST, WHIRLWIND, ANCIENT POWER, FUTURE SIGHT, HYDRO PUMP

Evolution:
Lugia does not evolve.

The ruler of the seas, Lugia spends its time deep at the bottom of the ocean because its powers are so amazingly strong. It is rumored to have been seen on the night of a violent storm.

Pokédex Pick:
New Pokémon like Marill, Elekid, and Lugia from Pokémon the First Movie: Mewtwo Strikes Back, and Pokémon the Movie 2000: The Power of One, are all residents of the Johto Universe!

Legend claims that this Pokémon flies the world's skies continuously on its magnificent seven-colored wings. A rainbow is said to form behind it when it flies through the crystal skies.

How to say it:
HO-oh

Type:
Fire/ Flying

Height:
12' 06"

Weight:
439 lbs.

Attacks:
SACRED FIRE, NORMAL, FIRE BLAST, SUNNY DAY, WHIRLWIND, ANCIENT POWER

Evolution:
Ho-oh does not evolve.

POKÉMON HALL OF FAME

Looks like Totodile is in LOVE!

Gligarman and his trusty Gligar come to Togepi's rescue!

Houndour heats things up.

Pineco and Brock make great friends.

YOUR FAVORITE POKÉMON IN ACTION

Scizor versus
Pikachu . . .
who will win?

Skarmory takes
to the air!

What could
Snubbull be
looking for?

Jessie is **NOT**
happy with
Wobbuffet!

Well, hello! I can see that you've learned all about the new Pokémon, bringing the grand total to 250 Pokémon! Hmmm...huh...wait a minute...according to my files...there should be a grand total of 251 Pokémon! Do you know what this means? There is still one more Pokémon out there that has yet to be discovered! Knowing this, are you sure that you can call yourself a Pokémon Master?

I am going to do something spectacular! I'm going to let you in on a little secret. Are you ready for this? Okay, I am going to tell you where you can find the **one remaining Pokémon.** It can be found in a huge forest, a monstrous forest that is lush and green, and full of ancient trees. You will immediately know when you have spotted this Pokémon, because it will be unlike anything you have ever seen. According to my sources, this Pokémon looks like a little alien or something. It appears to have some sort of bright streamers on its body, but what could it possible be?

I am certain that in time the future will reveal the secrets of this mysterious Pokémon. Until that time comes, continue practicing with your Pokémon, keep on growing, learning, and battling, and always be prepared for the next challenge.

Great meeting you, and I hope to see you again soon!

—Professor Oak

CHECKLIST:
HOW MANY OF THESE POKÉMON DO YOU HAVE?

❑ #01 Bulbasaur	❑ #41 Zubat	❑ #81 Magnemite
❑ #02 Ivysaur	❑ #42 Golbat	❑ #82 Magneton
❑ #03 Venusaur	❑ #43 Oddish	❑ #83 Farfetch'd
❑ #04 Charmander	❑ #44 Gloom	❑ #84 Doduo
❑ #05 Charmeleon	❑ #45 Vileplume	❑ #85 Dodrio
❑ #06 Charizard	❑ #46 Paras	❑ #86 Seel
❑ #07 Squirtle	❑ #47 Parasect	❑ #87 Dewgong
❑ #08 Wartortle	❑ #48 Venonat	❑ #88 Grimer
❑ #09 Blastoise	❑ #49 Venomoth	❑ #89 Muk
❑ #10 Caterpie	❑ #50 Diglett	❑ #90 Shellder
❑ #11 Metapod	❑ #51 Dugtrio	❑ #91 Cloyster
❑ #12 Butterfree	❑ #52 Meowth	❑ #92 Gastly
❑ #13 Weedle	❑ #53 Persian	❑ #93 Haunter
❑ #14 Kakuna	❑ #54 Psyduck	❑ #94 Gengar
❑ #15 Beedrill	❑ #55 Golduck	❑ #95 Onix
❑ #16 Pidgey	❑ #56 Mankey	❑ #96 Drowzee
❑ #17 Pidgeotto	❑ #57 Primeape	❑ #97 Hypno
❑ #18 Pidgeot	❑ #58 Growlithe	❑ #98 Krabby
❑ #19 Rattata	❑ #59 Arcanine	❑ #99 Kingler
❑ #20 Raticate	❑ #60 Poliwag	❑ #100 Voltorb
❑ #21 Spearow	❑ #61 Poliwhirl	❑ #101 Electrode
❑ #22 Fearow	❑ #62 Poliwrath	❑ #102 Exeggcute
❑ #23 Ekans	❑ #63 Abra	❑ #103 Exeggutor
❑ #24 Arbok	❑ #64 Kadabra	❑ #104 Cubone
❑ #25 Pikachu	❑ #65 Alakazam	❑ #105 Marowak
❑ #26 Raichu	❑ #66 Machop	❑ #106 Hitmonlee
❑ #27 Sandshrew	❑ #67 Machoke	❑ #107 Hitmonchan
❑ #28 Sandslash	❑ #68 Machamp	❑ #108 Lickitung
❑ #29 Nidoran♀	❑ #69 Bellsprout	❑ #109 Koffing
❑ #30 Nidorina	❑ #70 Weepinbell	❑ #110 Weezing
❑ #31 Nidoqueen	❑ #71 Victreebel	❑ #111 Rhyhorn
❑ #32 Nidoran♂	❑ #72 Tentacool	❑ #112 Rhydon
❑ #33 Nidorino	❑ #73 Tentacruel	❑ #113 Chansey
❑ #34 Nidoking	❑ #74 Geodude	❑ #114 Tangela
❑ #35 Clefairy	❑ #75 Graveler	❑ #115 Kangaskhan
❑ #36 Clefable	❑ #76 Golem	❑ #116 Horsea
❑ #37 Vulpix	❑ #77 Ponyta	❑ #117 Seadra
❑ #38 Ninetales	❑ #78 Rapidash	❑ #118 Goldeen
❑ #39 Jiggleypuff	❑ #79 Slowpoke	❑ #119 Seaking
❑ #40 Wigglytuff	❑ #80 Slowbro	❑ #120 Staryu

❏ #121 Starmie	❏ #164 Noctowl	❏ #207 Gligar
❏ #122 Mr. Mime	❏ #165 Ledyba	❏ #208 Steelix
❏ #123 Scyther	❏ #166 Ledian	❏ #209 Snubbull
❏ #124 Jynx	❏ #167 Spinarak	❏ #210 Granbull
❏ #125 Electabuzz	❏ #168 Ariados	❏ #211 Qwilfish
❏ #126 Magmar	❏ #169 Crobat	❏ #212 Scizor
❏ #127 Pinsir	❏ #170 Chinchou	❏ #213 Shuckle
❏ #128 Tauros	❏ #171 Lanturn	❏ #214 Heracross
❏ #129 Magikarp	❏ #172 Pichu	❏ #215 Sneasel
❏ #130 Gyarados	❏ #173 Cleffa	❏ #216 Teddiursa
❏ #131 Lapras	❏ #174 Igglybuff	❏ #217 Ursaring
❏ #132 Ditto	❏ #175 Togepi	❏ #218 Slugma
❏ #133 Eevee	❏ #176 Togetic	❏ #219 Magcargo
❏ #134 Vaporeon	❏ #177 Natu	❏ #220 Swinub
❏ #135 Jolteon	❏ #178 Xatu	❏ #221 Piloswine
❏ #136 Flareon	❏ #179 Mareep	❏ #222 Corsola
❏ #137 Porygon	❏ #180 Flaaffy	❏ #223 Remoraid
❏ #138 Omanyte	❏ #181 Ampharos	❏ #224 Octillery
❏ #139 Omaster	❏ #182 Bellossom	❏ #225 Delibird
❏ #140 Kabuto	❏ #183 Marill	❏ #226 Mantine
❏ #141 Kabutops	❏ #184 Azumarill	❏ #227 Skarmory
❏ #142 Aerodactyl	❏ #185 Sudowoodo	❏ #228 Houndour
❏ #143 Snorlax	❏ #186 Politoed	❏ #229 Houndoom
❏ #144 Articuno	❏ #187 Hoppip	❏ #230 Kingdra
❏ #145 Zapdos	❏ #188 Skiploom	❏ #231 Phanpy
❏ #146 Moltres	❏ #189 Jumpluff	❏ #232 Donphan
❏ #147 Dratini	❏ #190 Aipom	❏ #233 Porygon2
❏ #148 Dragonair	❏ #191 Sunkern	❏ #234 Stantler
❏ #149 Dragonite	❏ #192 Sunflora	❏ #235 Smeargle
❏ #150 Mewtwo	❏ #193 Yanma	❏ #236 Tyrogue
❏ #151 Mew	❏ #194 Wooper	❏ #237 Hitmontop
❏ #152 Chikorita	❏ #195 Quagsire	❏ #238 Smoochum
❏ #153 Bayleef	❏ #196 Espeon	❏ #239 Elekid
❏ #154 Meganium	❏ #197 Umbreon	❏ #240 Magby
❏ #155 Cyndaquil	❏ #198 Murkrow	❏ #241 Miltank
❏ #156 Quilava	❏ #199 Slowking	❏ #242 Blissey
❏ #157 Typhlosion	❏ #200 Misdreavus	❏ #243 Raikou
❏ #158 Totodile	❏ #201 Unown	❏ #244 Entei
❏ #159 Croconaw	❏ #202 Wobbuffet	❏ #245 Suicune
❏ #160 Feraligatr	❏ #203 Girafarig	❏ #246 Larvitar
❏ #161 Sentret	❏ #204 Pineco	❏ #247 Pupitar
❏ #162 Furret	❏ #205 Forretress	❏ #248 Tyranitar
❏ #163 Hoothoot	❏ #206 Dunsparce	❏ #249 Lugia
		❏ #250 Ho-oh